You Can Toucan

The Trinity Healing Method

Love, Pasha Lynn

The Trinity Healing Method

By
Pasha Lynn

The Trinity Healing Method
Copyright © 2017 Pasha Lynn. Produced and printed by Stillwater River Publications. All rights reserved. Written and produced in the United States of America. This book may not be reproduced or sold in any form without the expressed, written permission of the authors and publisher.
Visit our website at **www.StillwaterPress.com** for more information.
First Stillwater River Publications Edition

ISBN-10: 1-946-30015-2
ISBN-13: 978-1-946-30015-7

1 2 3 4 5 6 7 8 9 10
Written by Pasha Lynn
Cover Art by Rita Berkowitz
Published by Stillwater River Publications, Glocester, RI, USA.

The views and opinions expressed in this book are solely those of the author and do not necessarily reflect the views and opinions of the publisher.

This information is, in part, the root of all healing modalities including Western medicine. It has been channeled for those who are willing to engage themselves in a well-rounded healing modality.

As a student of level one, you are encouraged to practice as many steps in these pages that resonate with you.

As a level 1 practitioner, feel free to charge a price that you feel is reasonable.

Other healing methods believe that a practitioner transfers their energy to the student.

You are already the walking embodiment of The Great I Am.

And so it is!

Introduction

Welcome to your awakening. Congratulations on your decision to honor your birthright. It is my privilege to assist you on your journey.

Thank You!

Please know that all the knowledge, talent, and abilities that will be discussed in these pages, already exist inside your mind, heart, and soul.

This program is designed to help you unlock your abilities, to help you find your power and creativity, and to foster the courage necessary to use your magical gifts.

You will learn an Old Brilliant Original Understanding that is so critical it will change the world at this time.

This will be a much-needed relief for a society that is too focused on materialism and media!

I recommend this form of healing to those who are in need of modifying patients, loved ones, or themselves, so that all can reach their highest potential.

And so it is!

Love Pasha Lynn

Basic Concept of This Class

The focus of this class is to learn how to practice Energy Medicine which centers around the energy field called the aura.

The aura is made up of three parts: energy meridians, chakras, and energy bodies.

When one system is out of balance, there is a chemical and electrical surge that affects the human energy field. This can be proven by using a thermography camera.

The human body emits a ray of radiation that is measured at about one hundred watts. This energetic field submission is used in medical imaging.

Thermography uses an infrared camera to visualize the pattern of emissions which cannot be detected by the human eye, but can be detected or experienced as heat.

Thermography can detect acute and chronic inflammatory conditions. This method is documented by many research studies, showing toxic accumulations, tumors, and other diseases.

All human bodies are made up of bio-fields. Every field has a different frequency within the electromagnetic spectrum that emits from the body.

These emissions can be proven by the Kirlian Effect.

Bio-field therapy, such as Trinity Healing, begins treatment by sensing imbalances in the individual, then it improves their energy regulations by transmitting energy to the loved one using many different electromagnetic fields. This is also known as E.M.F.

My Biography

I began life on November 2, 1961 in Los Angeles, California.

My mother was 20 years-old and had given birth to my sister 14 months earlier. She was learning the hard way that motherhood is one of the most difficult jobs, and certainly one she was not prepared for at the time. In her absence, I learned to walk, and talk in my crib. Therefore, I learned to astral project at a very young age.

In truth, I feel as though I chose her for that very reason.

One of the first turning points in my young life was in 1982 when I traveled to Israel.

I wish I knew how to express the experience I had during this time. The only way to explain what occurred may make me sound a bit delusional.

In fact, I once told the story to a rabbi, and he told me that I must have been hallucinating at the time.

If it wasn't for a cross that I was handed after I was enlightened, I might have agreed with him.

Needless to say, I have been walking with the information that Spirit is going to awaken those who seek out the primal connection to the light and energy of the creator, and it is this unique spiritual role that will be transmitted in these pages.

Of course, my biography doesn't end there.

My personal reawakenings have occurred time and time again.

It occurred once by a rebbe in 1990 (a rebbe is a master teacher of the Torah.) Another time, it was by the Peruvian healers at the White Light Bookstore in Cranston, Rhode Island.

Another enlightening message came from Roland Comtois. Roland is a spiritual medium. Roland announced to about 200 people at an opening of a church on Rose Street in Providence that I was a gift from heaven. Messages like these are delivered by such miraculous souls to validate the intention of Spirit.

Another validation was by a man who asked me to call him Uncle. He owns an Indian store on Thayer Street in Providence. He began telling me about how he had come to live in RI. It was a conversation that I will never forget even though he did all the talking. He stated that he was there to motivate me, to engage my contract. He said that I was here to affect the world by helping others release their old belief systems that limit their abilities. He encouraged me to speak the universal truth, that we are all one -- we are the same! He told me it was time to express my knowing of the fact that every cellular system boils down to a frequency. A megahertz, if you will. Everything is equivalent. For every action, there is a reaction. Opposites attract, but there are still monopoles. Energy cannot be created or destroyed. There is no Death, only transition! Afterward, he gave me free Indian food, and a box of gluten free cookies. He then explained that he knew I was a Celiac, and that I would enjoy these cookies later during the day with a cup of tea. They would be the best cookies that I have ever eaten. He was right!

I have since realized that the reasons for the simple gifts -- the food, the cross and Israel -- were tools used by Spirit so that I had a physical validation of the experience.

Then there was John of God at the Omega Center. John of God is a spiritual healer from Brazil. I went to see him in New York and he took 80 of us aside and said, through his interpreter, that we were all fully-awakened human beings. He explained to us that the time has come for us to reeducate those willing to receive. He concluded that we need to go back to our rooms so that Spirit could enlighten us.

In Brazil, I lived one miracle after another. That left me with a feeling of awe, that Spirit could enlighten us. We were asked not to speak to others for 24 hours: not to read, or watch TV, or even listen to the radio. We were not to engage in any other activities. We should only drink blessed water.

Being of sound mind, (ha, ha, ha...) I answered the phone when my son called, and as soon as I walked out of the room, I engaged in a conversation with a man who recognized me. Then I found my girlfriend who asked me to go out to lunch. When I stopped and asked someone for directions to the lunchroom, the whole ground began to shake. I felt as if I was going to pass out. So, I went back to my room.

What I learned...

You're awakening begins whether you are ready or not.

      Believe!

As of a few weeks ago, I thought that my biography would end with John of God.

      However...

While taking a class, called "Journey of the Soul." I was told that my Soul was fully integrated. That tidbit of information was expressed to me by the same rabbi who told me that I must have been hallucinating, after I told him about the incident in Israel.

      I think I have come full circle.

      Therefore, I say to you.

      "It is now time for you to begin your journey."

      And so it is!

A burning bush at my wedding.
I didn't see it until I was looking at the photo a few years ago.
Look closely and you will see a dove flying out of the flames.

A Bridge

A bridge is an object

that allows you to continue on your chosen path

while passing over obstacles.

Washing of the hands

A cleansing of oneself and a bond with your educator.

Water is a symbol of Life. When washing our hands, our intention should be directed toward renewing oneself in a variety of settings: cleansing spiritually, and physically, for the work ahead.

Biofield

Biofields are many energy pathways in, on, and around the human body.

They are the flow of energy that every Life form encompasses.

Chakras are constantly spinning vortexes of energy, which radiate from the spinal column.

There are seven primary chakras that run vertically through the center of the body.

The aura is comprised of several layers of energy they are commonly known as the Physical, Etheric, Emotional, Mental, and Spiritual Bodies.

The Physical body has seven energy layers around it.

The biofield is dynamic and ever changing. At any given time, they may vary in frequency, energy, and depth depending on our physical health, thoughts, and feelings.

Pictured is Katherine Wheeler, owner of The Greatful Heart on West Main Street in Wickford, Rhode Island demonstrating her chakra camera. Through a technology known as Kerlian photography this camera helps us visualize our human energy.

Protection

In order to protect oneself, the negative and positive flow of qi -- or the human electrical system – can be used to create a circuit.

Each finger (except for the thumbs) has a polarity. Your first digit is negative, your second digit is positive, and so on for the last two fingers.

In order to create the circuitry, you must join the negative to the positive fingers.

The thumbs join together creating a triangle formation.

Practicing this technique will help this formation to become automatic.

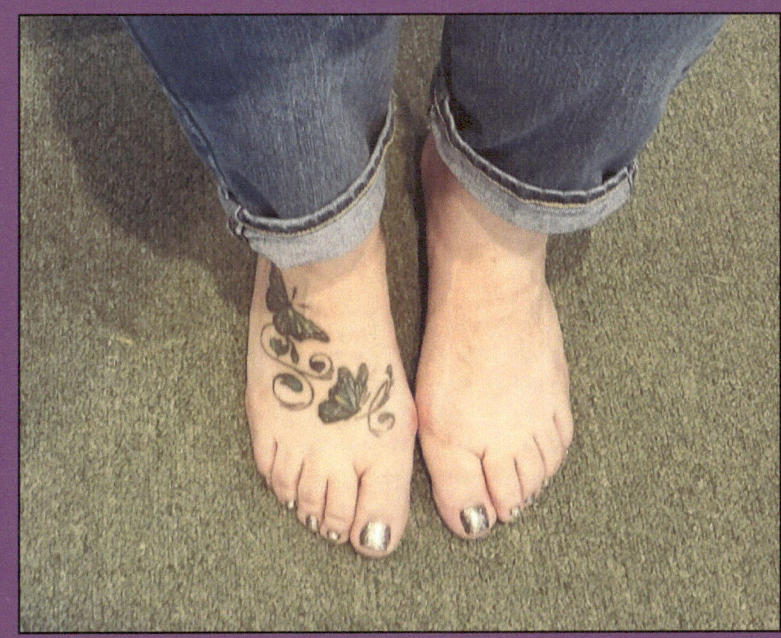

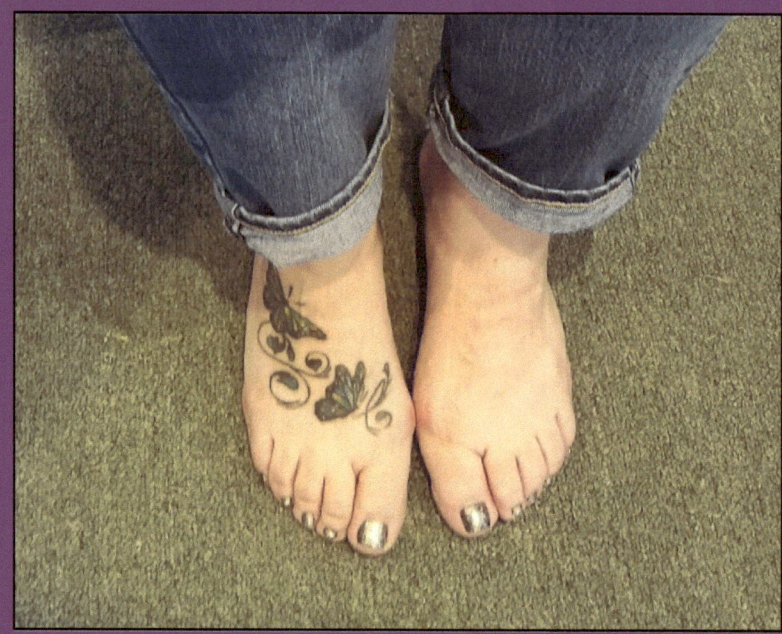

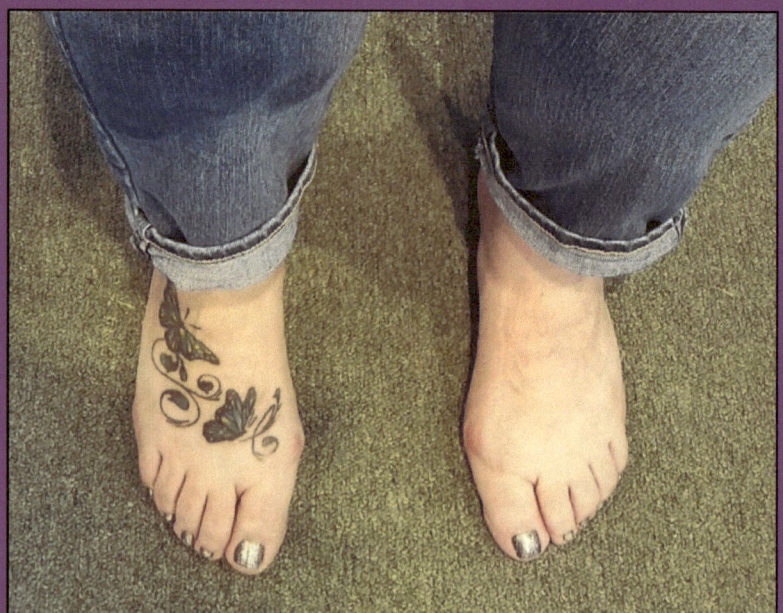

American Blessed Soup

4 bouillon cubes
1 can tomato juice cocktail
1 large potato diced
2 carrots sliced
2 stalks of celery diced
1 can of diced tomatoes
1 cup chopped fresh green spinach
1 cup fresh corn kernels
salt and pepper to taste
Creole seasoning to taste

Kumbucha

In traditional medicine, the application of kumbucha showed such positive results that labels such as "magic" and "miracle" became associated with it.

What is kumbucha? It is a naturally carbonated, fermented tea. It is an ancient drink made for centuries and celebrated for its health benefits. It is said to have originated in China during the Tsin Dynasty, around 221 B.C., where it was nicknamed the "elixir of life."

Kumbucha has many health benefits. When you drink it, Kumbucha binds with the minerals in your body to create and encourage alkalinity. It boosts your immune system, and it is a natural detoxifier.

Kumbucha is known to increase your metabolism, to boost your energy, and also to relieve arthritis and joint pain. It is rich in antioxidants, and contains vitamins and enzymes.

In addition to beneficial bacteria, Kumbucha contains B vitamins that provide support for the body's metabolic function including overall energy, utilization of carbohydrates, heart health, and healthy hair, skin, and nails. Adequate intake of B vitamins can reduce stress, anxiety, and depression, boost memory and relieve PMS.

During the 1980s, President Ronald Reagan drank one liter of Kumbucha daily to prevent the spread of colon cancer. His success was noted.

Hippocrates said, "death sits in our bowels" which links many illnesses to problems with digestion. According to experts, the healing of bowel flora is the first and most important step to curing any illness.

We are what we eat (and drink).

Energy Cleaning a Room

When cleansing a room, you may evoke the use of many implements including but not limited to, incense, oils, herbs, candles, bird feathers, music, and crystals.

The use of crystals is ideal because some clients are affected by the use of certain mediums.

A good intention with the focus of charging the room with positive energy is the ideal thought process. Don't underestimate the power of intention. You need not believe in the power of your tools but believe in the efficacy of your intention.

Thoughts carry a lot of energy!

I have been told to open windows. This allows the negative energy to leave the space.

Don't forget to clean the nooks and crannies.

Energetically cleansing your space leaves you with a delicious feeling of fulfillment.

Vibrational Frequency

Everything in the universe vibrates! Every atom, every molecule, every element!

This bioenergy also known as qi (chi) or life force can be measured in hertz.

A healthy human body has a daytime frequency in the range of 62 to 68 MHz

Dr. Royal Raymond Rife (1888-1971) conducted research with a machine he developed called a "frequency generator." With the use of this machine, he concluded that every disease has a specific frequency.

According to Dr. Rife, every cell, tissue and organ has its own vibratory resonance. Working with his frequency generator, he found that specific frequency will destroy a cancer cell or a virus. His research demonstrates that certain frequencies could also prevent the development of disease, and that other frequencies would neutralize disease.

A radiologist by the name of Bjorn Nordenstrom, from Stockholm Sweden, discovered in the early 1980s that by putting an electrode inside a tumor and running a milliamp of direct current through the electrode, he could dissolve a cancer tumor and stop its growth. He also found that the human body had electropositive and electronegative energy fields.

With this knowledge of frequency, we can prevent illness by altering our exposure to negative energy fields.

In conclusion, if we manipulate our environment so that it has a positive vibrational frequency, we will be less likely to develop certain illness.

Meditation

A basic definition of meditation is to engage in contemplation or reflection; to engage in mental exercise (as concentration on one's breathing or repetition of a mantra) for the purpose of reaching a heightened level of spiritual awareness.

The Loved One's Part

Another important aspect!

The possibility exists that the biofield will shift due to a transient thought or action.

In order to avoid a rebound effect, we must educate the loved one.

The loved one will receive, however they must participate in the outcome by avoiding certain stimulus that may affect the embodiment of the spiritual being.

Hence, in order for them to receive their intention, we ask for them to meditate and avoid media including reading (if at all possible). Included in these recommendations, there is an additional requirement that the said soul eliminate, for a recommended time of 30 days, the following: ingesting spicy foods, drinking alcohol, smoking, crowds, and any other Energetic Therapies. (Because the individual is now very open to other people's influences.) Also avoid medications except those prescribed by a doctor, and refrain from sex.

Basically, anything that raises the energetic field of a loved one should be avoided!

The prescribed amount of time varies from person to person. It usually will last for 30 days.

A psychic surgery can spontaneously occur during and post intervention.

It helps to be aware of this information.

See the energy that appeared in the photo after it was taken.
It was sent at 2:22. The Trinity at work.

Picking a New Name and the Rebirth Process

Letting go of one's birth name has value to a spirit for the reason that said soul is taking charge of oneself. A given name no longer serves you. Changing your name allows you to take control of a self-propelled destination, inviting your soul to start anew.

A rebirth offers one's self a chance to open up a new and welcomed path, no longer sidestepping the old emotions that bind you. You now have a new prospective. You will nurture your inner child. You will receive the nourishment that is your birthright. You will successfully open the door to your imagination. You will fall in love with your innocence and your playfulness.

You will become increasingly aware of your authentic self.

And so it is!

Qi Life Force

Music affects the life force of energy. This is also known as Qi. In fact, all forms of energy are interchangeable. This is also the scenario with color, chakras, aromas, foods, elements, senses, associated glands, and thought itself.

Every item on this list has an equivalent, as described in the chart on the following pages.

That is to say, every sound has an energetic vibration, smell, taste and color.

These relationships are defined by Einstein's theory in 1905. $E=Mc^2$.

Simply stated, energy is equal to mass times the speed of light squared.

This equation helps explain the application of universal physics, and for the expression in our cosmic existence.

Splining Open a Chakra

Splining open a chakra is a definition describing how to access a portal, or passageway, to a chosen chakra.

A chakra spins clockwise from the front to the back, also known as anterior to posterior.

In order to open up a chakra, one would only have to reverse the polarity. In other words, it means to move the energy in a counterclockwise motion.

This is easily achieved by using a crystal going in a counterclockwise motion. Using a crystal creates a transference of electrons in the electrical field.

Once the chakra is opened, you can use the crystal to pull any condensed energy that may reside in the chakra.

Picturing a fireplace in your mind's eye, toss the energy from the crystal into the fire and allow it to burn up. Visualize the fireplace. Feel the heat. Believe,

and so it is.

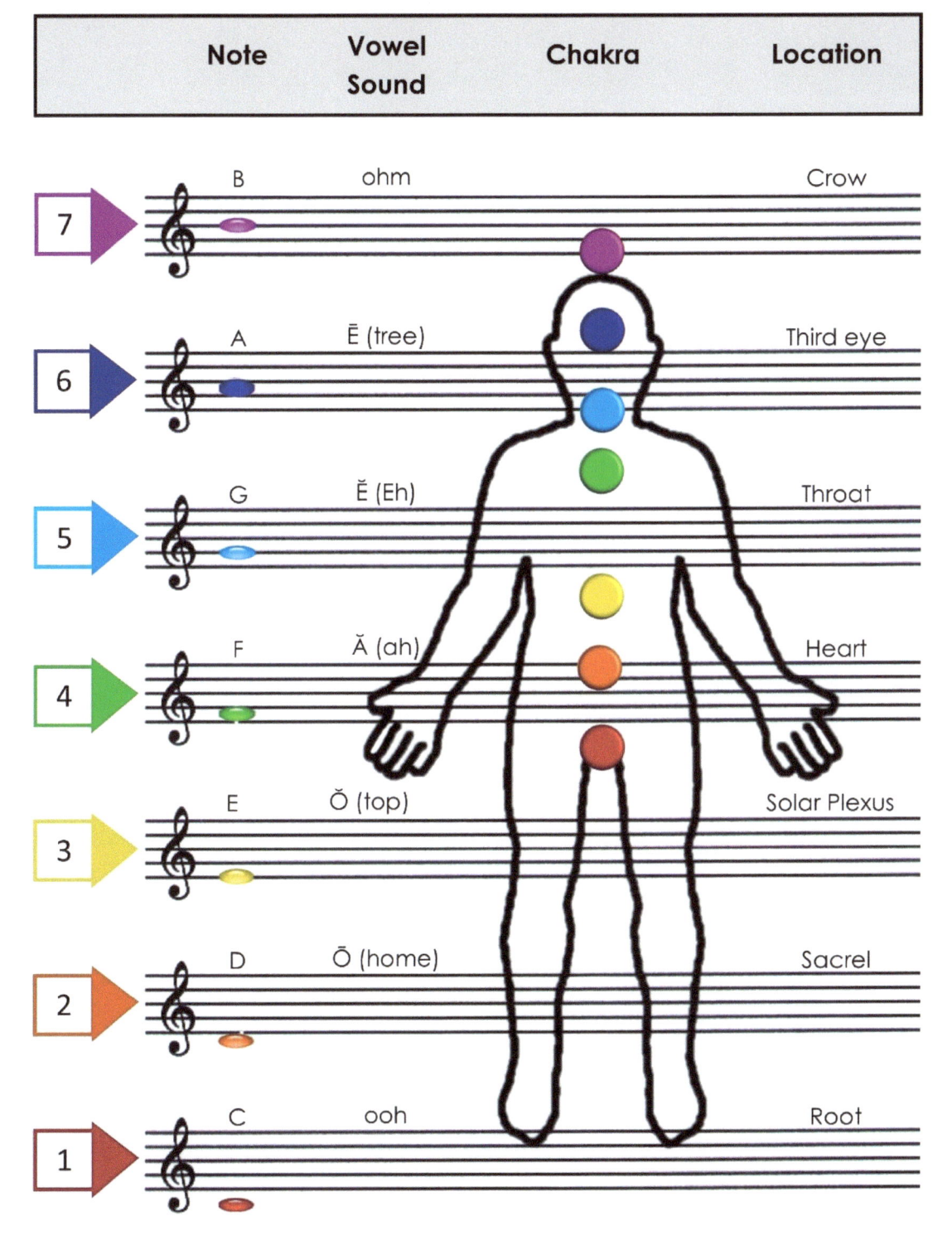

Foods

● Broccoli, beet tops, blackberries, eggplant, and purple grapes.

● Both blue and violet foods.

● Asparagus, blueberries, plums, and potatoes.

● Avocados, beans, broccoli, cucumbers, green peppers, lettuce, olives, peas, spinach, and zucchini.

● Bananas, corn, grapefruit, eggs, lemons, parsnips, pineapple, yams, and yellow peppers.

● Apricots, carrots, mangoes, oranges, peaches, persimmons, pumpkins, and tangerines.

● Beets, cherries, red cabbage, red peppers, red plums, strawberries, tomatoes, watercress, and watermelon.

Aromas

- 🟣 Rose, lotus, olibanum, and spruce.

- 🔵 Jasmine, mugwort, star anise, and mint.

- 🔵 Eucalyptus, frankincense, sage and benzoin.

- 🟢 Rose oil, yarrow, orris root, and marjoram.

- 🟡 Bergamot, carnation, rosemary, and lavender.

- 🟠 Gardenia, sandalwood, and Damian's ylang-ylang.

- 🔴 Cedar, pepper, clove and vetiver.

Qualities and Functions

○ Universal consciousness, perfection, bliss, unity with the divine being, wisdom and purpose, enlightenment and understanding

○ Intuition, clairvoyance, extrasensory perception, concentration, peace of mind and manifestation.

○ Self-expression, truth, communication, integrity, wisdom, and confidence.

○ Compassion, understanding, warmth, unconditional love, forgiveness, healing, sincerity, devotion, and selflessness.

○ Vitality, personal power, social identity, authority, self-control, energy, radiance, joy, will, peace, acceptance of self, action, and influence.

○ Sexuality, desire, pleasure, enthusiasm, relationships, union with nature, openness to others, personal creativity, primal feelings, procreation.

○ Trust, courage, grounding, power to achieve goals, satisfaction, and material security.

Element Senses

 Thought

 Light

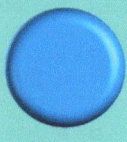 Ether/Sound

 Air/Touch

 Fire/Sight

 Water/Taste

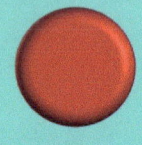 Earth/Smell

The Essential Point of a Trinity Healing Practice is Dependent on the Incorporation of an Enlightened Soul.

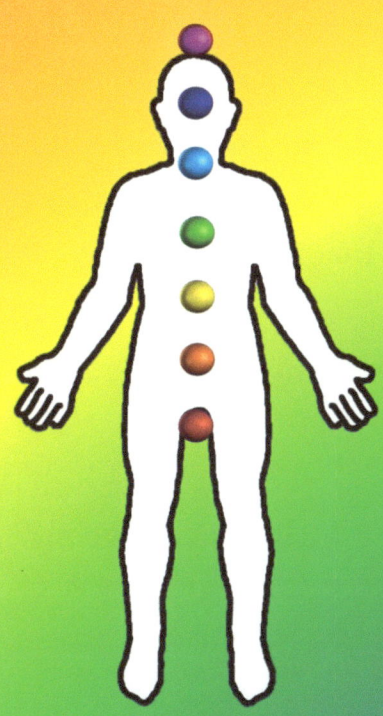

I have experienced this through my personal ability to astral-travel.

My belief is that everybody experiences things differently.

Being empathetic, clairvoyant, and clairaudio, I am often left with verbal messages and or physical impressions of my clients. My best explanation of a healing session is I'm on the outside viewing my physical body as though it were a hologram. It never hurts, but if necessary, a spirit allows me to feel a twinge in the area of my client's body that needs addressing.

I am left with an impression or a knowing.

One of my clients received news from a spirit who would incarnate as her son. She had recently divorced and didn't see that in her near future. Seven years later, she gave birth to a beautiful healthy boy.

In order to relate the message intended for the client, spirit engaged my soul talent.

Note: This was not the issue the client came in for. Spirit is in tune to all needs of the client.

Allowing another soul to incorporate in your human form is a blessing.

I can only state that as long as you remain unattached to the outcome of a healing session, and have the highest intention for the client or loved one, you are honoring your role.

You are allowing spirit to use you as a conduit. We are the facilitators of the healing session, not the healers. Yet, we are a vital part in the circuitry. Spirit works through you for the highest good.

The Reconnection Shake

Reconnecting spiritually is a birthright. This process allows you to enjoy the energy grid which consumes every object on this planet. Once opened, your dormant DNA is awakened and you will receive an influx of universal frequencies, allowing you to enjoy life and information that eluded you prior to your dimensional upgrade.

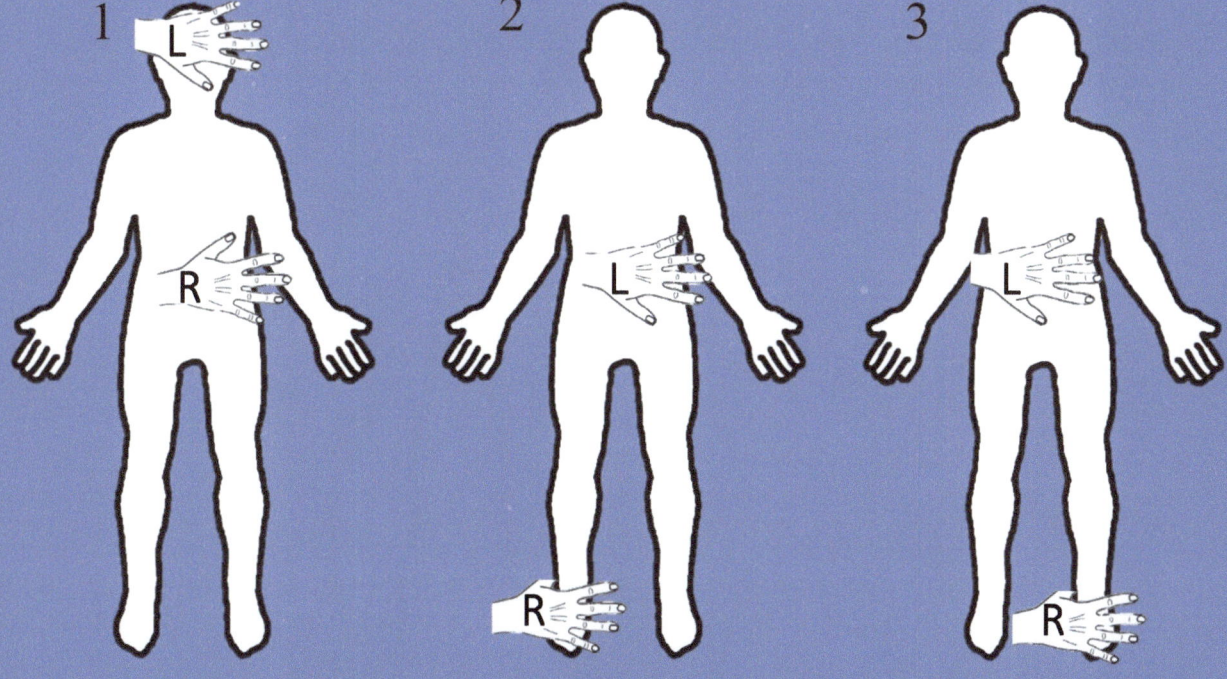

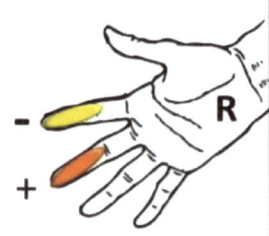
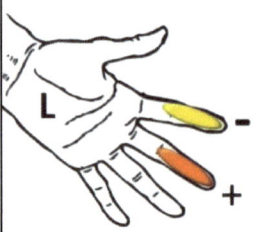

Meridian Snake

The Meridian Snake is a sacred grid, a representation of the human polarity system. Performing the Meridian Snake entices your natural electrical current to switch on like a light switch.

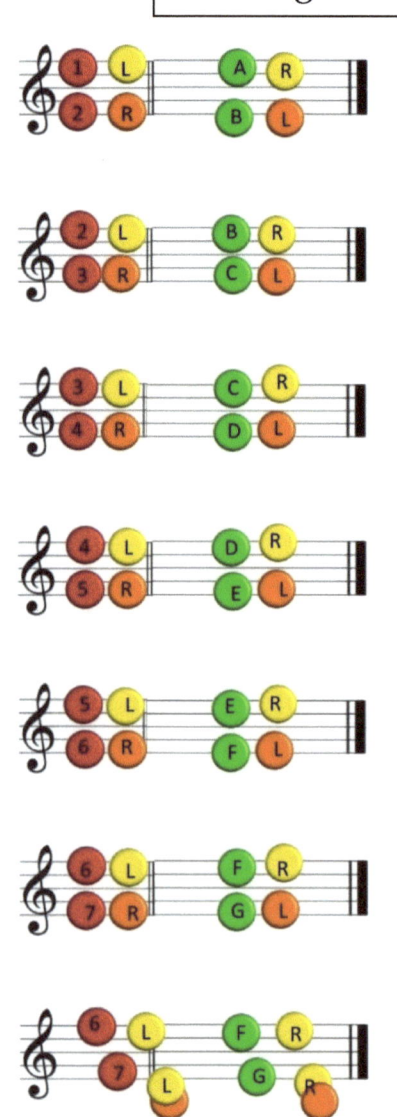
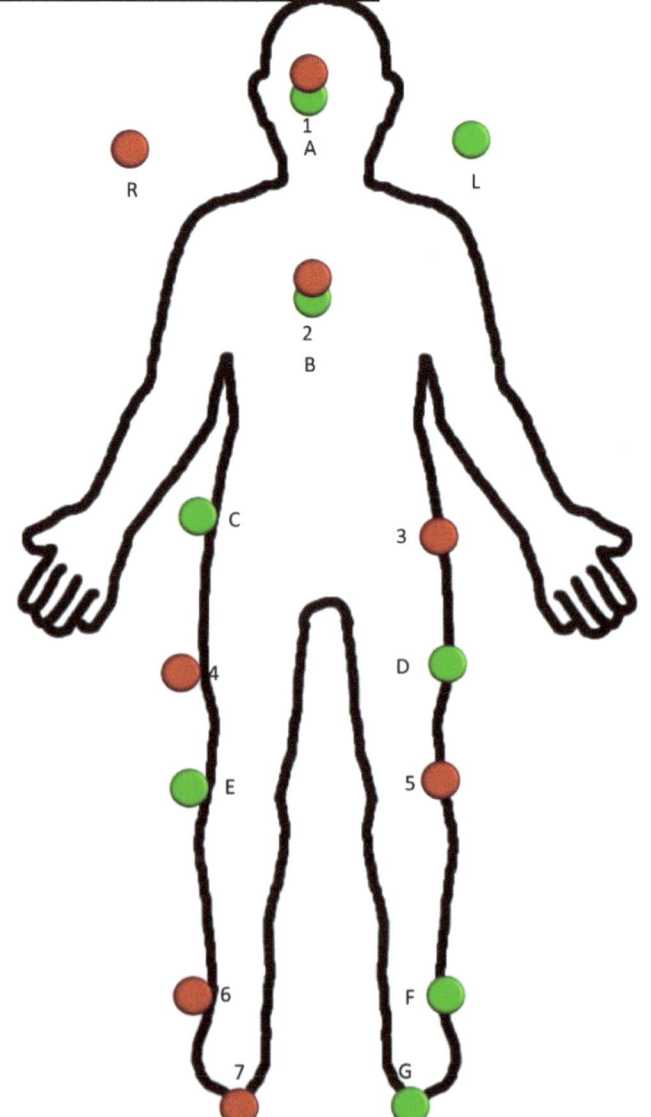

The Trinity Sweep

The Trinity Sweep connects the client to the cosmos, yet at the same time, it has a grounding effect.

The facilitator presents their hands in a perpetual meridian current, connecting the loved one to the universal grid, enveloped in the Earth and our atmosphere.

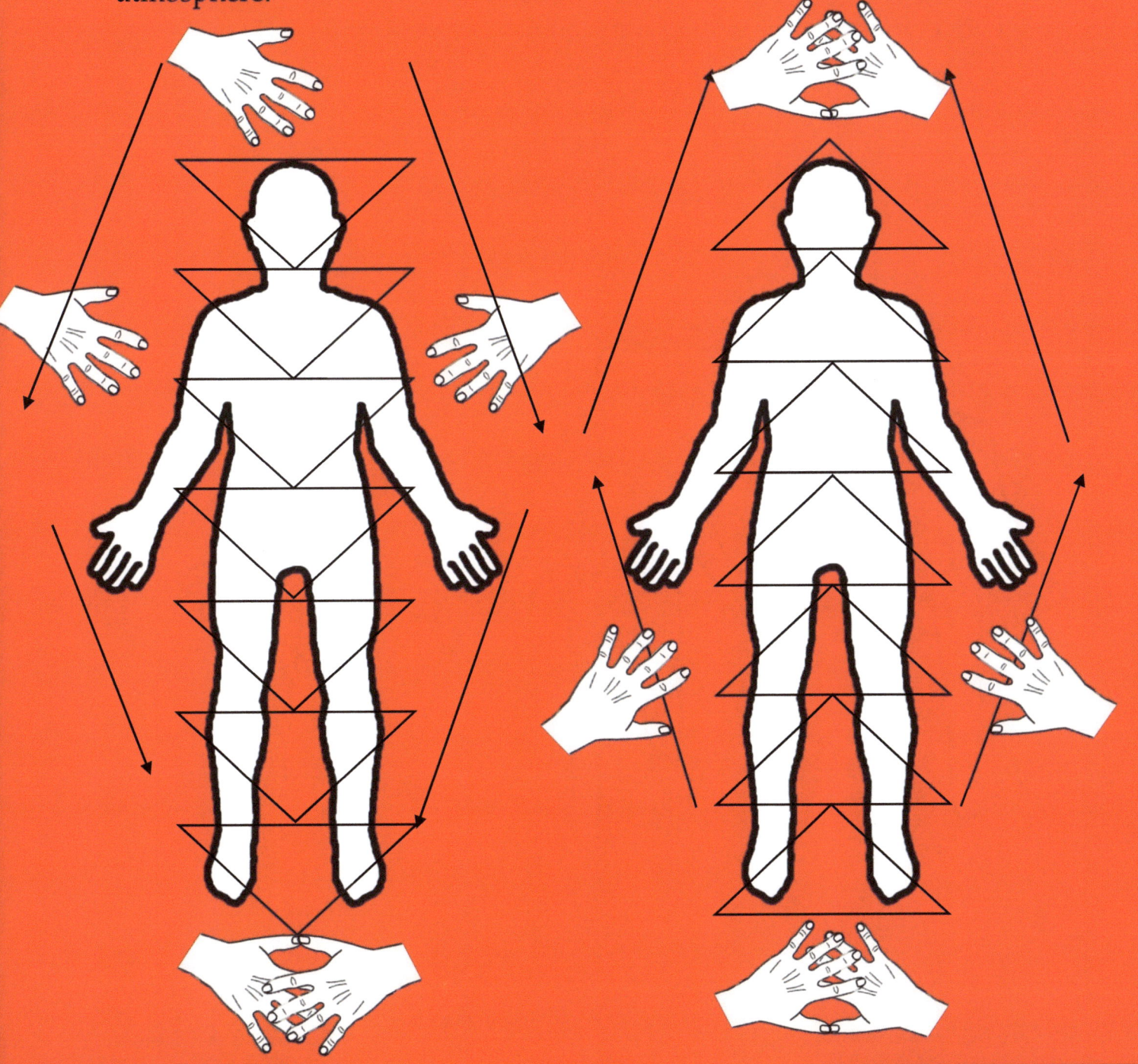

The Finale

Reconnection Shake

The last step to the Trinity Healing Process is the same as the reconnection shake.

Think of it as a hand shake.

You are again connecting their magnetic field, tying it all together, embracing them if you will. The energy transference is very unique and special!

This is where you peak as a true spiritual vibration!

And so it is. (Namaste)

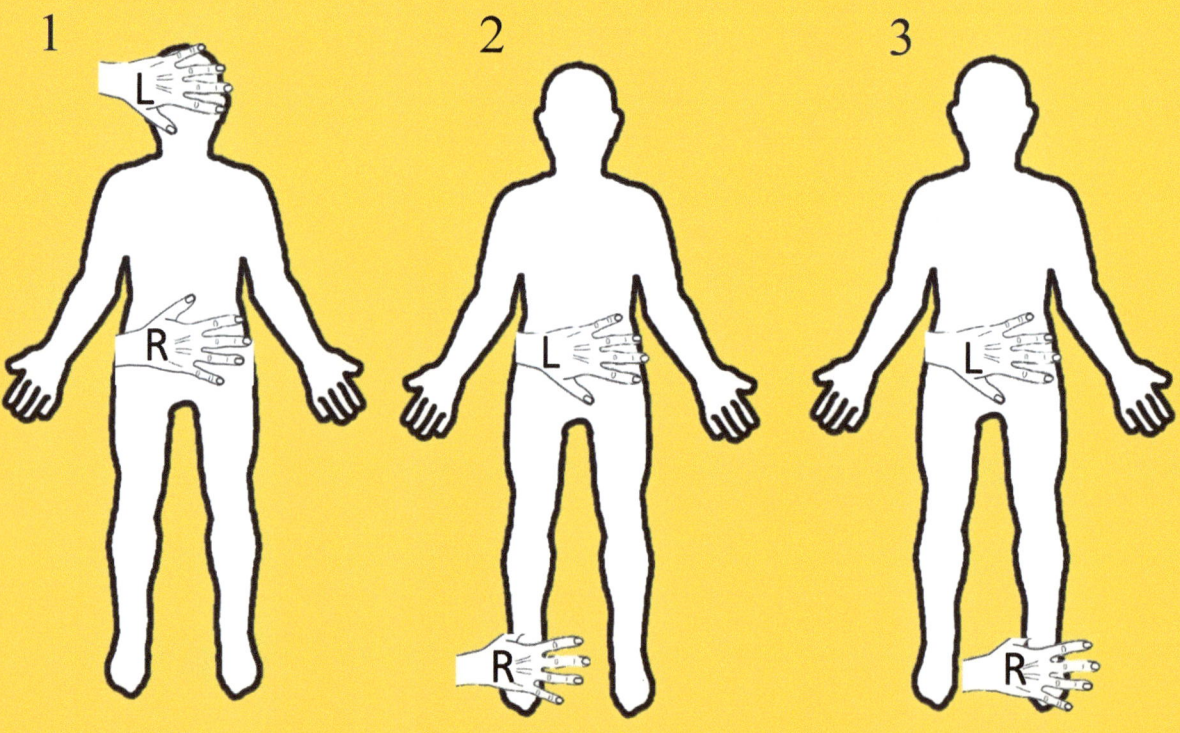

Finding Your Soul Talent

Finding your soul talent is the same as finding your authentic self.

A soul comes into this world with a specific talent whether it be clairvoyance, (clear seeing or psychic vision), clairaudience, (clear feeling, sensing or psychic feeling, or clairempathy), clairtangency (clear touching or commonly called psychometry), claircognizance (clear knowing or psychic knowing), clairgustance (clear tasting or psychic tasting, sometimes also called clairambience), clairalience (clear smelling or psychic smelling, sometimes also call clear-scent).

To help you recognize your soul talent, know that it is a natural ability that you have been walking with since birth.

If one is naturally clairvoyant, you may be more attuned to paying attention to how things look. Learning comes naturally to you if there are visuals.

If you are someone who loves to sing, play a musical instrument, or write music, sounds call to you. You are more apt to be clairaudient.

If you tend to focus on how things physically and emotionally feel to you during your day, this may indicate that you are clairsentient.

A sense of enjoyment received from knitting or writing can be considered clairtangency.

A knowing that somebody is about to call is a sign that you may be claircognizant.

Someone whose passion includes cooking or drinking wine may have been born with clairgustance.

Those who are blessed with clairalience love to stop and smell the roses.

All of these special abilities help us to receive information that will indeed help a loved one during a healing session.

I encourage you to reach beyond the limitations and self-doubt that hold you back from using your psychic abilities.

Manifest your heart's desire using your intuition.

Everything was threes! The Trinity again.

Candles

Candles are used in nearly every major religion. The word candle is derived from the Latin word "candera" which roughly translates to mean "to shine."

When enhanced with a color and fragrance, candles produce the same effect on the chakra system as it's celebrated equal.

Candles light your way to heaven.

Oils and Incense

Oils and incense are great tools to help with spiritual harmony and to align your physical and mental self.

Oils and incense have been around for centuries and help bring balance to your chakra system.

- Frankincense: One of the most spiritually charged oils. It has been around for thousands of years and brings us peace and clarity.

- Lavender: Incredibly calming and great for headaches. Helps to achieve a higher state of consciousness.

- Eucalyptus: helps clear sinuses and cure a sore throat or cough allowing free and clear self-expression.

- Rose: enhances romance and love. It is also helpful for alleviating depression and insomnia.

- Cinnamon: Allows you to heat up your power center.

- Sandalwood: Releases your desire. Aids as an aphrodisiac.

- Patchouli: Enhances a sense of security and stability. Grounds you.

Saying Prayers and Affirmations

Since we know that every sound has a vibration, a color, and a smell, we can understand the relationship between thought and the spoken word.

Taking this mindset into account, we can also conclude that our own personal relationships with the creator generate a physical attunement.

Indeed, we become the cellular activity of thought itself.

That being said, we can acknowledge the fact that when we enter the personal space of our loved ones, and engage them, we in turn effect their own cellular activity. This is called "tanking" and was written by Dr. Barbara Barbach in 1995.

As you can see, a positive and uplifting prayer and affirmation increases your ability to stimulate and effect everything and all that is.

Affirmations and Prayers

I Am

I am now consciously living my divine purpose.

I am one with the divine source.

I See

I am creative.

I am positive.

I am perfectly attuned to my vision.

I Speak.

I express my thoughts and feelings clearly and effectively.

I express myself freely and easily.

I Love

I am a channel for divine love.

I am an expression of love.

I put my heart into everything I do.

I Can

I am full of energy and radiate light.

My personal power is growing stronger every day.

I accept myself completely.

I Feel

I feel I am able to create transformation.

I feel my creativity streaming through my body.

I open myself to others naturally.

I Have

I have unshakable trust.

I am safe and secure.

I am rooted in life and in myself.

Gemstones

Each gemstone has its own unique personality, energy and vibration. Like petals on a flower, they will provide you sustenance, and beauty.

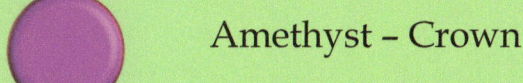 Amethyst – Crown

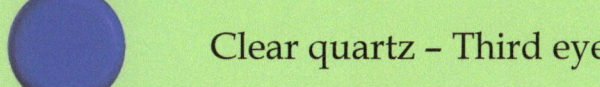 Clear quartz – Third eye

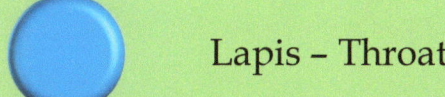 Lapis – Throat

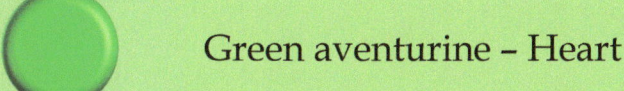 Green aventurine – Heart

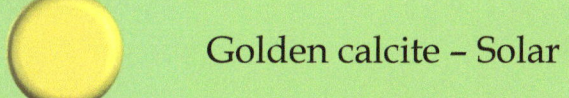 Golden calcite – Solar

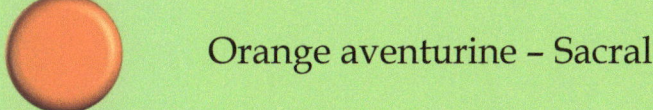 Orange aventurine – Sacral

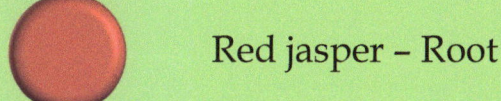 Red jasper – Root

Last Thoughts

As this chapter comes to a close, my thoughts drift back to the day that spirit used my voice to enlighten Rabi Laufer off a faulty fuse in a conversion van that we had given him. After three hours of the Rabi's trials and tribulations, he broke down and tested the fuse that spirit originally stated was at fault. And that was the reason the car was not starting. (And yes, it was the fuse.)

My thought about the outcome is that it did not matter who received the information. The only important thing is there were souls that benefited from the operation of the vehicle.

And so it is!

P.S. We are all just vehicles!

Love, Pasha

Dedication

This is the fun part where I get to thank every soul living, and otherwise.

I'm not sure how to do it without first saying that I'm grateful for every person that crosses my path. I am always surprised by the lessons that I have learned from a neighbor or a flight attendant.

Those wonderful people whom I love and adore!

Ron, Steph, and Ben. You have taught me patience, humility and how to party like it's 1999. You have truly supported my being. And of course, corrected me when I used phrases like, "woo, woo." I am the luckiest!

To my beautiful sister-in-law and my Auntie Susan. You taught me how to fly. You gave me wings.

My besties. I love each and every one of you!

Aviv for all the wise things you say! Erin for your angelic soul! Linda – Wow – beautiful funny and smart! You're a gift! Of course, my soul-sister Mary – my ray of sunshine! Sometimes it's like looking in a mirror! You are my split art! Richard, who makes me fall down with laughter every time I see him! Steve – a – la. Where would our lives be without you? Mark – you're quiet as a mouse but your heart is huge!! Dr. Dave, I love to love you!

My silly Bro Jeff – you have always been there for me! You're my sounding board and friend. I love you!

I also need to give a shout out to Vicky and Michelle for helping me to pull things together. Thank you.

Love   and   😘   Pasha Lynn

Don't weep, don't cry.

I am not gone. I'll never die.

My soul is free, it travels in the sky,

It lives in the wind and survives with love and beauty.

I am not dead.

I have only ended one chapter of life, and went on to the next,

and when your soul joins mine you will see that life is like a line

that goes on forever.

No, I will never die.

My soul will be free, it will travel in the sky,

live in the wind and survive with love and beauty.

This is a poem channeled on October 9, 1977 at 3 a.m. It was written by Maxwell Shieff, a famous clothing designer and documented psychic in Beverly Hills, California, who passed unexpectedly. This poem was written for his sister to recite at his eulogy.

Congratulations! You have completed your first step in the progression of being a registered Trinity Healer. 😇

Your second degree is a phone call away.

This will allow you to practice as a second degree registered Trinity Healer.

We encourage you to charge money, and or barter for your services. At this junction, an exchange of energy is very important for the loved one to experience the energy on an equal plateau. (Note: If working on a child, ask them to allow you to hold their favorite toy for 15 minutes.)

To receive your second degree certification, we will invite you to an online class and a free video chat with a third degree master.

You will also receive a certificate of authenticity and registration in our national directory.

Call now to register to become a second degree practitioner.

(401) 965-8057. 8 a.m. to 5 p.m., Monday -Friday, eastern time

www.ingramcontent.com/pod-product-compliance
Lightning Source LLC
Chambersburg PA
CBHW042014150426
43196CB00002B/44